THE HISTORY PUZZLE

CHERRY DENMAN

THE HISTORY PUZZLE

Turner Publishing, Inc.

ATLANTA

Library of Congress Cataloging-in-Publication Data
Denman, Cherry.
   History puzzle: an interactive visual timeline / illustrated by Cherry Denman.
     —1st ed.
     p. cm.
   Summary: Panoramas present events and people in world history, from the
     dawn of life to the edge of tomorrow. Clues challenge readers to create their
     own interactive timeline.
   ISBN 1-57036-200-9 (alk. paper)
   1. Chronology, Historical—Juvenile literature. 2. World history—
     Chronology—Juvenile literature. [1. World history] I. Title.
   D11.D385 1995
   372.89'044—dc20   95-17537
                                        CIP
                                        AC

Published by Turner Publishing, Inc.
A Subsidiary of Turner Broadcasting System, Inc.
1050 Techwood Drive, N.W.
Atlanta, Georgia 30318

Distributed by Andrews and McMeel
A Universal Press Syndicate Company
4900 Main Street
Kansas City, Missouri 64112

First Edition 10 9 8 7 6 5 4 3 2 1

Printed in China

for
Barnaby

THE HISTORY PUZZLE

Putting Together
The History Puzzle

Just about everybody enjoys figuring out a good jigsaw puzzle. Trouble is, when you're all done, what do you have? A pretty picture—and nothing more. Putting together the History Puzzle is different. For every name of a person or event you match to a picture in the puzzle, you will have learned something about your world, your past, and yourself. That's the fun of history: seeing how you fit into time.

The best way to work the History Puzzle is to look at one two-page spread at a time and try to match the printed clues at the bottom of the pages with the figures pictured in the spread.

The clues are in alphabetical—not chronological—order. Use a pencil to mark the pictured figures and events with the number of the clue that matches. Or, if you don't want to mark your book, simply record the name of each figure and event you identify on a separate piece of paper. You can

4,600
million years ago

600
million years ago

play alone. Or you can play with mom, dad, sister, brother, and friends—and see who can identify the most figures and events.

The History Puzzle is of special interest to Americans because the last six two-page spreads focus on the history of our nation. But don't forget the spreads that come before! These tell the story of our mother country, England—going back thousands, even millions of years, long before England or America existed as nations and even long before people appeared on the earth. Running along the bottom of each scene, you will find figures and events from many other parts of the world.

Each of the hundreds, even thousands of figures and events pictured in *The History Puzzle* has a fascinating story to go along with him, her, or it. Turn to the end of the puzzle for a short list of books that will tell you more. Following that, you will also find a complete answer key. No peeking!

500
million years ago

400
million years ago

300
million years ago

Here are the clues:
1 Ammonite: giant shell
2 Diplocaulus: its oddly-shaped head kept it from being easily swallowed
3 Gemuendina, Dinichthys, Bothriolepis: fish with jaws
4 Meganeura: giant dragonfly
5 Nautiloid: some were cone shaped
6 Pteraspis, Drepanaspis, Hemicyclaspis, and Birkenia: the first fish
7 Starfish: just like today's animal
8 Trilobite: ancestor of shrimps and lobsters

1 Alexander the Great (356–323 B.C.): conquered the known world
2 Aristotle (384–322 B.C.): Greek thinker
3 Beaker people: so called from their drinking vessels
4 Buddha: India's "Enlightened One"
5 Julius Caesar (100–44 B.C.) : Rome's greatest leader
6 Celts: blonde, blue-eyed

7 Cleopatra (69–30 B.C.): Queen of Egypt, 51–30 B.C.
8 Confucius (551–479 B.C.): Chinese philosopher
9 Cuneiform: the first writing
10 Dinosaur eggs: round or sausage shaped
11 Druids: priests, teachers, and administrators
12 Edaphosaurus: had sails on its back

13 The first farms
14 The Great Pyramid: Giza, Egypt
15 Great Wall of China: 1,500 miles long
16 Homo Habilis: first true human being
17 Maiden Castle, Dorset: Britons fought invading Celts
18 Megalosaurus: a fearsome predator

19 Migration from Asia to America, 10–50,000 years ago
20 Moses: led the Exodus, 1250 B.C.
21 Oldest Briton: Swanscombe man (280,000 years old)
22 Olmecs: first known American civilization
23 Plateosaurus: commonest early dinosaur
24 Plato (428–348 B.C.): Greek thinker

25 Primitive crocodile
26 Procompsognathus: fed on insects and early mammals
27 Pterosaur: first flying animal after insects
28 Smilodon: saber-toothed cat
29 Stegosaurus: brain the size of a walnut
30 Stonehenge: Salisbury, England

31 Triceratops: best-known horned dinosaur
32 Turtle: like the modern one
33 Venus de Milo: famous statue without arms
34 Woolly mammoth: as large as an army tank
35 Ziggurat at Ur: stepped pyramid built by the Sumerians

1 Agricola (A.D. 40–93): Roman governor of Britain (with wheat sheaf)
2 St. Alban: first British martyr
3 The Antonine Wall: built by Romans
4 Boadicea: led a bloody revolt against the Romans

5 Caligula (A.D. 12–41): Roman emperor—made his horse a consul
6 Chandragupta: united Northern India
7 Claudius I (10 B.C.–A.D. 54): brought elephants to impress the British
8 Constantine I (306–337): made Christianity the Roman imperial religion
9 Cunobelin: with the coin of Cymbeline; two sons: Togodumnus and
  Caractacus

10 Hadrian (A.D. 76–138): Roman emperor built a wall to keep the Picts
   out of Britain
11 Hopewell Indian mounds of North America
12 St. Jerome: translator of the Bible

13 Jesus Christ
14 Prince (or Princess) Liu Sheng: buried in a suit made of
    2,498 pieces of jade
15 Magnetic compass used in China
16 The Missing Ninth Roman Legion: disappeared in Britain
17 Nero (A.D. 37–68): Rome burned during his reign

18 Paper invented in China
19 Picts and Scots breaking down Hadrian's Wall
20 Roman dwellings
21 Roman road builders
22 The Romans leaving Britain

23 The Sack of Rome: Visigoths led by Alaric
24 Saxons arriving along the East Coast
25 "The Tortoise" (Testudo): Roman assault formation
26 Vespasian (A.D. 9–79): Roman invader of Britain
27 Eruption of Mt. Vesuvius in Italy, buried Pompeii

1 Acropolis of Zimbabwe built, A.D. 850
2 St. Aidan: founded Lindisfarne, source of the Lindisfarne gospels
3 Alcuin (with book under arm): a great English scholar
4 Aldfrith the Learned: king of Northumbria and great teacher
5 Ambrosius Aurelianus: at Battle of Mount Badon, 520
6 King Arthur at Tintagel
7 Attila the Hun: invader of Gaul and Northern Italy
8 King Athelfrith: of Northumbria, 593
9 King Athelric: created kingdom of Northumbria, 588

10 St. Augustine: first Archbishop of Canterbury, 601–604
11 St. Benedict (480–547): founder of the first monastery
12 Buddhism: introduced to Japan, 552
13 Caedmon: greatest of early English poets
14 Ceawlin (in purple, with staff): West Saxon king.
15 King Cenwulf of Mercia, 796
16 Cerdic and Cynric: kings of the West Saxons, 519
17 Charlemagne (742–814): crowned Roman Emperor, 800
18 Clovis I: founder of the Frankish kingdom, 486

19 St. Columba: Irish island missionary, 563
20 King Cuthwulf of the West Saxons
21 St. Cuthbert: had a pet seal who turned the pages of his book
22 Dome of the Rock of Jerusalem finished, 692
23 Edwin of Northumbria, ruled 616–632
24 King Egbert and his Witan (council): first king of *all* England
25 King Ethelbert and Queen Bertha of Kent, ruled 560–616
26 Ethelburga: married Edwin of Northumbria, thereby spreading
   Christianity north
27 Kings Ethelwulf (died 858), Ethelbald (ruled 856–860), Ethelbert
   (ruled 860–866), Ethelred I (ruled 866–871)

28 Gildas: poet who wrote about the invaders
29 The Great Mosque, Cordoba, 788
30 Hengist and Horsa: hired to fight off the Picts, 449
31 Abbess Hilda: maintained a famous abbey at Whitby
32 King Ine, of the West Saxons, with *Ine's Code*, earliest collection
   of West Saxon laws. With him, Bishop Ealdhem
33 Emperor Justinian (483–565): reconquered the Western Empire
34 Man reading *Beowulf*, the first English epic poem
35 Mayan civilization in Central America

36 Mercian Kings Ethelred (died 716) and Ethelbald (died 757)
37 Muhammad: founder of Islam
38 King Offa of Mercia: with coins
39 Oswald: second son of Athelfrith, carried a wooden cross into battle
   against Cadwallon
40 St. Patrick of Ireland
41 Paulinus: accompanied Ethelburga on her journey north
42 Penda and Cadwallon: heathen allies against King Edwin
43 Playing cards invented in China, 696
44 Pope Gregory I (590–604)

45 Printing invented in China
46 Saxon symbols for the days of the week
47 Sutton Hoo: ship burial near Ipswich, Suffolk
48 St. Swithin: with cloud and sun
49 Theodore of Tarsus: a Greek monk sent from Rome to keep England
   in the Roman way of Christianity, 668; with Hadrian of Carthage
50 Venerable Bede: "Father of English learning"
51 King Wulfhere of Mercia

1 **King Aethelstan:** Edward the Elder's son, handsome with long golden hair
2 **King Alfred and Queen Ealhswith:** "the king who burnt the cakes"
3 Alfred founded a school at Winchester; Grimbald ran it
4 King Alfred's men hiding in the marshes after the defeat at Chippenham, 878
5 Archbishops Odo and Wulfstan
6 **Avicenna:** great Persian physician (980–1037)
7 **Berserker** (with shield and axe): a wild warrior Viking

8 **Cahokia:** North America's first city, about 990
9 **Canute the Great:** king of England, Denmark, and Norway; famous for getting his feet wet to show his courtiers that he was not all-powerful
10 **Hugh Capet:** first of a French royal line that lasted nine centuries
11 **St. Dunstan:** important statesman and music lover
12 Battle of Edington: victory over the Danes
13 **King Edgar the Peaceful:** eight vassal kings rowed him across the River Dee to show their acceptance of him as their overlord

14 **King Edmund Ironside:** Ethelred's son, who died in 1016
15 **King Edmund:** stabbed to death by a robber, Leofa
16 **St. Edmund:** Vikings shot him with arrows
17 **King Edred:** with broadsword and scepter
18 **King Edward the Confessor:** built the first Westminster Abbey
19 **King Edward the Elder:** fought the Danes and was helped by his sister Ethelfleda, a great warrior
20 **King Edward the Martyr:** murdered in 978
21 **Edwy the Fair:** quarreled with Dunstan about his relationship with the beautiful Aelhelgifu

22 Ethelred the Unready (968–1016): under his weak rule, England was
   swamped by new Danish invaders

23 Lady Godiva: rode naked through the streets of Coventry

24 Gunhild: saw her husband and child butchered in St. Brice's Massacre
   (ordered by Ethelred)

25 Baptism of Guthrum: defeated at Edington, Guthrum agreed to
   baptism

26 Hardicanute: quarreled with his brother Harold I (Harefoot)

27 Harold I (Harefoot): King of England, 1035–40

28 Hastinga (with winged helmet): Viking warrior

29 Ivar the Boneless (with shield and dagger): captured
   Northumbria in 866

30 Kettle Flatnose and Olag the Fart: two famous Vikings

31 Leif Ericsson: discovered America, 1000

32 Othere: Alfred's explorer, who discovered the Land of the
   Midnight Sun

33 German king Otto I: became Holy Roman Emperor, 962

34 Rhazes: great Arabian physician

35 First known stained-glass window, Augsburg Cathedral,
   Germany, 1065

36 King Sweyn "Forkbeard" of Denmark: drove Ethelred into exile, 1003

37 Last Tang emperor deposed in China, 907

38 Tollan: became the capital city of the Toltecs, in Mexico

39 Uffington white horse

40 Vikings discovered Iceland, 860

41 Prince Vladimir of Kiev: Christianized Russia, 988

42 Good King Wenceslas: Bohemian king celebrated in the
   Christmas carol

1 Alp Arslan: established a large Turkish empire, 1071

2 Bishop Anselm: Archbishop of Canterbury, 1093–1109

3 The Crusades (red cross symbol): First Crusade, 1095–1099

4 Second Crusade: 1147–48

5 *William's Doomesday Book:* a record of everyone living in England around 1086

6 Easter Island Heads: carved from soft volcanic stone between 1000 and 1600

7 Holy Roman Emperor Frederick I (called Barbarossa): led the Third Crusade, 1189–92

8 Hardrada and ally Tostig: King Harold promised Hardrada "just six feet of our land, for his grave."

9 Harold Godwine: killed by an arrow above the right eye in 1056

10 Henry I: Became king on the death of his brother Rufus; taxes were counted out on a checkerboard

11 Henry I: died from eating too many lampreys, 1135

1150

12 Hereward the Wake: William smoked his followers out by setting fire to the rushes

13 Queen Matilda: surrounded by King Stephen's men in Oxford castle; escaped by rope

14 Bishop Odo of Bayeux with the great Bayeux tapestry

15 The Rise of the Samurai: Japanese warrior class

16 King Stephen (1097–1154): Matilda should have succeeded him, but Stephen disputed her claim; war broke out

17 Henry I's only son, William, died in the wreck of the White Ship, 1120

18 Pope Urban II (ca. 1035–99): launched the Crusades

19 William the Conqueror (1028–87): crowned during a snowstorm on Christmas, 1066, and built the Tower of London; he "laid waste to the North" to punish rebellion; he saw Halley's comet and took it as a sign that he would defeat the English; he tripped and fell, then stood up with both hands full of earth—"Look, I have seized England with my two hands."

20 William II (1056–1100): succeeded William the Conqueror; known as Rufus because of his red hair; killed by an arrow through the neck

1 Al Idrisi: Arabian scholar produced a flat map of the world
2 Angkor: ancient temple city of Cambodia
3 Arthur: son of Richard I's dead brother Geoffrey; should have been heir to the throne, but John Lackland had him blinded and castrated
4 Thomas à Becket: disputed with Henry II over Church authority
5 Queen Berengaria of Navarre, wife of Richard I: the only queen of England who never set foot there

6 Blondel: Richard's faithful minstrel
7 Canterbury Cathedral, built in the twelfth century
8 Children's Crusade, 1212
9 Fourth Crusade, 1198–1204
10 St. Dominic: founder of the Dominican order of friars
11 Eleanor of Aquitaine: later imprisoned by her husband Henry

12 Explosives first used in China, 1161
13 St. Francis of Assisi: founder of the Franciscan order
14 Genghis Khan (1162–1227): conquered much of China, Persia, Poland, India, and Russia
15 Henry II (1133–89): square, thick-set, bull-necked, bandy legged, short red hair, freckled; great king

1215   1225   1250

1 St. Thomas Aquinas (1224–74): one of the Middle Ages' most brilliant
  thinkers
2 Roger Bacon (1220–92): early Englishman of science
3 John de Balliol (1249–1315): king of Scotland; forced to abdicate in 1296
4 Blue knight: a knight Hospitaller; Red Cross knight; a Teutonic knight;
  White Cross knight: a Knight Templar
5 Fifth Crusade, 1216–21: in Egypt
6 Sixth Crusade, 1228: led by Frederick II
7 Seventh Crusade, 1248–52: led by Louis IX

8 Dante (1265–1321): wrote the *Divine Comedy*
9 King Edward I, "Longshanks" (1239–1307): renowned for dispensing
  good justice and strengthening parliament
10 Edward I's Welsh castles: displayed the art of castle-building at its best
11 Queen Eleanor (1246–90) and Baby Edward II: Edward I promised
  the Welsh a new prince who would speak no English; he accordingly
  gave his infant son the title of Prince of Wales
12 Eleanor of Provence (1223–91): wife of Henry III and taller than he
13 Eleanor's crosses: in 1290, Queen Eleanor of Castile died; Edward I
  had twelve stone crosses erected in her honor

14 Elephant: gift to Henry III from Louis IX of France
15 Eustace the Monk: English Channel pirate
16 Eyeglasses invented in Italy, 1290
17 Frederick II, Holy Roman Emperor (1194–1250): recovered
  Jerusalem in 1229
18 Giotto (1267–1337): Italian painter
19 Robert Grosseteste: first chancellor of Oxford University
20 King Henry III (1207–72): stocky and unpopular
21 Hubert de Burgh: justiciar who ruled England after the death of
  William Marshal

22 Incas: rise in Peru

23 Expulsion of the Jews from England, 1290: Jews had to wear two strips of yellow cloth to identify themselves

24 Knight's armor: so heavy that some knights had to be hoisted into their saddles by means of a winch

25 Kublai Khan (1215–94): led the Mongol conquest of China, 1279

26 Llewelyn: last independent Prince of Wales

27 King Louis IX of France (1214–70): St. Louis

28 William Marshal, Earl of Pembroke (star badge): regent for young King Henry II

29 First mirrors, 1280

30 Pandolf the Papal Legate and Peter des Roches, the king's tutor and Bishop of Winchester: quarreled with Hubert de Burgh

31 Matthew Paris: great chronicler based in St. Albans

32 John Pecham: Archbishop of Canterbury, 1279–92

33 Marco Polo (1254–1324): traveled to China, 1271–95

34 Provisions of Oxford: created a kind of parliament, 1258

35 Robert the Bruce, Earl of Carrick: after suffering defeat, he learned a lesson in determination by watching a spider

36 Sheep: wool was England's major source of revenue

37 Simon de Montfort: rebelled against his brother-in-law

38 Stone of Scone: Edward I captured the Scottish Stone of Destiny, on which Scottish kings were crowned; stone still lies under the British Coronation Chair

39 William Tell: shot an apple off his son's head

40 Timbuktu: capital of the Muslim kingdom of Mali, West Africa

41 Sir William Wallace (1270–1305): led the Scottish resistance

42 Westminster Abbey: Henry III rebuilt the West Abbey

1 Aztecs in Mexico
2 The Black Death: carried in the bloodstream of the black rat and transmitted by its fleas
3 Giovanni Boccaccio (1313–75): great Italian storyteller
4 Geoffrey Chaucer (1340–1400): wrote the *Canterbury Tales*
5 Emperor Chu Yuan-Chang: founded the Ming Dynasty in China, 1368
6 English bowmen: won the Battles of Crécy and Poitiers
7 Duccio di Boninsegna: painter from Siena, Italy (1250–1319)

8 King Edward II (1284–1327): killed by order of Isabella, "the she-wolf of France"
9 Edward III (1312–77): over six feet tall, "a new Arthur"
10 Edward, the Black Prince (1330–76): chivalric knight who married Joan, "the fair maid of Kent"
11 Piers Gaveston: Edward II's favorite knight
12 Duke of Gloucester and Henry Bolingbroke: powerful, feared, and ultimately murdered

13 Hugh Despenser the Elder and Hugh Despenser the Younger: favorites of Edward II; hung, drawn, and quartered in 1326
14 Ibn Battuta: Arab geographer; explored the Sahara Desert
15 Isabella I (1451–1504): raised an army in France to invade England and overthrow Edward II
16 Jeanne de Belleville: a Breton lady pirate
17 John of Gaunt (1340–99): father of the future King Henry IV
18 William Langland: wrote *Piers Ploughman*, early English literary classic, 1362

19 Mansa Musa: king of Mali
20 Jacques de Molay: master of the Knights Templar
21 Osman I: Turkish sultan; founder of the Ottoman empire
22 Alice Perrers: Edward III's last mistress; politically powerful
23 Peter de la Mare: first speaker of the House of Commons, 1376
24 Petrarch (1304–74): writer of beautiful sonnets
25 Philip the Fair (1268–1314): king of France
26 Philippa of Hainault: Edward III's queen, who bore twelve children

27 Plague doctor: "beak" stuffed with herbs to filter the air
28 Red Rose of the House of Lancaster
29 King Richard II (1367–1400): died of starvation in Pontefract Castle;
   even his greyhound, Matt, deserted him
30 The great schism between Rome and Avignon, France: rival Popes
   elected
31 Walter Stapledon, Bishop of Exeter: dragged from his horse and
   decapitated with a kitchen knife
32 Tamerlane (1336–1405): Mongol emperor

33 Wat Tyler and John Ball: led the Peasant's Revolt, 1381
34 Earls of Warwick and Lancaster: plotted Piers Gaveston's murder,
   1312
35 William of Wykeham: founded Winchester College and
   New College, Oxford
36 John Wycliffe (1330–84): reformed the Church in England

1 Battle of Agincourt, 1415
2 Dukes of Bedford and Gloucester: Henry V's brothers
3 Brandy invented in Modena, Italy, 1450
4 Filippo Brunelleschi (1377–1446): great Italian architect
5 Jack Cade: leader of a mob rebellion in London

6 Catherine of Aragon: daughter of Charles VI of France who married Henry V
7 Charles VI of France (1368–1422): a maniac
8 Cheng Ho (1405–33): Chinese explorer who made seven voyages to India, Persia, and Africa

9 The Dauphin: son of Charles VI of France
10 Eton school founded, 1440
11 Owen Glendower: incited Wales to rise up against Henry IV
12 Gutenburg Bible printed about 1455
13 Prince Henry the Navigator (1394–1460): Portuguese monarch and explorer

14 Henry IV (1366–1413): wife was Joan of Navarre

15 Henry V (1387–1422): great warrior king who died young

16 Henry VI (1421–71): suffered from insanity

17 Jan Hus (1372–1415): Czech religious reformer burned at the stake

18 St. Joan of Arc (1412–31): told by God to save France

19 Lollards burned as heretics, 1401

20 Margaret of Anjou (1430–82): battled Duke Richard of York for the throne in the War of the Roses

21 Montezuma I (1440–68): ruler of the Aztecs

22 A Native American

23 The Earl of Northumberland and his son, Harry Hotspur: revolted against Henry VI

24 Sigismund (1368–1437): Holy Roman Emperor who visited London on a peace mission, 1416

25 Dick Whittington: rags-to-riches Londoner

26 Chinese scholar Yung-lo: compiled an encyclopedia of 22,937 volumes, 1403

1 Sandro Botticelli (1445–1510): painter of the famous *Birth of Venus*, 1458
2 William Caxton: brought the printing press to England
3 Charles the Bold, Duke of Burgundy

4 Duke of Clarence: betrayed his brother Edward IV and died in a butt (barrel) of Malmsey wine
5 King Edward IV (1442–83): reigned 1461–83
6 King Edward V (aged twelve) and his brother Richard (nine): held in the Tower of London and murdered

7 Ferdinand and Isabella of Spain
8 Duke of Gloucester (Richard III): ordered the murder of King Henry VI
9 Lord Hastings: beheaded without a trial for opposing Richard III
10 Ivan III (1440–1505): founder of Moscow and first czar of Russia

11 Warriors of the Japanese civil wars, 1467–1568
12 Kano Masanobu (1434–1530): great Japanese artist
13 Louis XI (1423–83): king of France
14 Sir Thomas Malory: English author of *Morte d'Arthur*
15 First printed music in Europe, 1465

16 Richard III (1452–85): deformed and nasty king of England
17 Richard, Earl of Warwick (1461–71): a leader of the House of York
18 Lord Rivers and his nephew Grey
19 Lord Stanley: picked up slain Richard III's crown at Battle of Bosworth Field, 1485

20 Sunni Ali: ruler of the Songhai people in West Africa, 1464
21 Prince of Wales: stabbed by Duke of Gloucester (Richard III), 1471
22 Elizabeth Woodville, Lady Grey: married Edward IV in secret, 1464

1 Anne Boleyn: Henry VIII's second wife
2 Anne of Cleves: Henry VIII's fourth wife
3 Prince Arthur, Henry VIII's elder brother: his death (1502) made
   Henry VIII heir to the throne
4 Robert Aske: led a revolt against the new Church of England
5 Babur (1483–1530): first Muslim Mogul ruler of India
6 First globe made by Martin Behaim, 1492
7 Lucrezia Borgia (1480–1519): famous poisoner
8 Hiëronymus Bosch: grotesque Dutch painter
9 John Calvin (1509–64): started Protestant movement in Switzerland
   and France, 1536
10 Catherine of Aragon (1485–1536): Henry VIII's first wife
11 Emperor Charles V (1500–58): Holy Roman emperor

12 Christopher Columbus (1451–1506): sailed to America, 1492
13 John Colet (1466–1519): Oxford scholar and Church reformer
14 Nicolaus Copernicus (1473–1543): Polish astronomer, declared that
   the earth revolves around the sun
15 Hernán Cortés (1485–1547): conquered the Aztecs, 1521
16 Thomas Cranmer (1489–1556): Archbishop of Canterbury under
   Henry VIII
17 Thomas Cromwell: advisor to Henry VIII; beheaded in 1540
18 Thomas Culpepper: Catherine Howard's cousin and lover
19 Albrecht Dürer (1471–1528): great German artist
20 Elizabeth of York: married Henry VII
21 Erasmus (1466–1536): most learned man of the Renaissance
22 Field of the Cloth of Gold: pageant staged to impress the French
   king, 1520

23 St. John Fisher: executed for refusing to swear an oath of loyalty to
   Henry VIII, 1535
24 Francis I of France (1494–1547): a knightly king
25 Henry VII (1457–1509): beat Richard III at the battle of Bosworth
   Field, 1485
26 Henry VIII (1491–1547): most famous king of England (reigned
   1509–47)
27 Hans Holbein the Younger (1497–1543): German painter hired by
   Henry VIII
28 Catherine Howard (1520–42): Henry VIII's fifth wife
29 Ivan the Terrible (1530–84): bad Russian czar
30 James IV of Scotland: killed in the Battle of Flodden Field, 1513
31 James V of Scotland: died, leaving the kingdom to the infant Mary,
   Queen of Scots

32 Leonardo da Vinci (1452–1519): painted the *Mona Lisa*, about 1502

33 Lorenzo de' Medici, "Lorenzo the Magnificent" (1449–92): powerful Florentine

34 St. Ignatius of Loyola (1491–1556): Spanish founder of the Jesuits, 1534

35 Martin Luther (1483–1546): nailed his 95 "theses" to the church door at Wittenberg, starting the Protestant Reformation

36 Niccolò Machiavelli (1469–1527): author of *The Prince*, about ruthlessness in politics, 1513

37 Magellan: initiated first voyage around the world, 1519–21

38 Margaret: Henry VII's daughter; married King James IV of Scotland

39 *Mary Rose* wrecked, 1540

40 Mary, sister of Henry VIII: married Louis XII of France

41 Michelangelo Buonarroti (1475–1564): painted the Sistine Chapel

42 Monasteries: closed by Henry VIII, 1536–39

43 Sir Thomas More (1478–1535): executed for refusing to swear an oath of loyalty to Henry VIII

44 John Morton, Bishop of Ely: extorted money from the wealthy—with a fork

45 Catherine Parr (1512–48): sixth and last wife of Henry VIII

46 Sir Edward Poynings: gave English Parliament power over the Irish Parliament, 1494

47 François Rabelais: author of *Gargantua* and *Pantagruel* (about 1534)

48 Savonarola (1452–98): influential Florentine reformer; burned as a heretic

49 Jane Seymour (1509–37): Henry VIII's third wife

50 Lambert Simnel and Perkin Warbeck (son of a boatman): claimed to be two princes presumed murdered in the Tower of London

51 African slaves taken to America

52 Mark Smeaton: executed as Anne Boleyn's lover

53 Battle of the Spurs, 1513: so called because the French ran away so fast

54 Süleyman the Magnificent: great Ottoman sultan

55 William Tyndale: and his great English Bible, 1539

56 Vasco da Gama: sailed to India around Cape of Good Hope, 1498

57 First pocket watch: made in Germany

58 Cardinal Thomas Wolsey: Henry VIII's unscrupulous advisor

1 Ahmed Al Mansur: leader of the Moroccans
2 Akbar the Great (1542–1605): greatest of the Mogul emperors
3 Sir Francis Bacon (1561–1626): English lawyer, courtier, author, statesman, and philosopher
4 Earl of Bothwell: married Mary, Queen of Scots shortly after Lord Darnley's death
5 Peter Brueghel (1525–69): Flemish painter
6 William Byrd (1543–1623): organist and great composer
7 Edward Campion (1540–81): tried to restore Catholicism to England
8 Catherine de' Medici (1519–89): taught the French how to cook
9 Robert Cecil (1563–1612): son of Lord Burghley; advisor to James I
10 William Cecil, Lord Burghley (1520–98): Elizabeth I's great advisor
11 Lord Darnley (1545–67): Mary, Queen of Scots' husband, who murdered her Italian secretary and friend, David Rizzio

12 Robert Devereux, Second Earl of Essex (1566–1601): favorite of Elizabeth; executed for treason
13 John Dowland (1562–1626): great lute player and composer
14 Sir Francis Drake (1542–96): greatest sailor of his age
15 Drake's Drum: beats whenever danger threatens England
16 John Dudley, Duke of Northumberland: replaced Edward Seymour, Duke of Somerset, 1549
17 Robert Dudley, Earl of Leicester (1532–88): favorite of Elizabeth I, but hated by others
18 Edward VI (1537–53): sickly son of Henry VIII
19 Elizabeth I (1533–1603): England's great queen
20 John Foxe (1516–87): wrote *Book of Martyrs*
21 Sir Martin Frobisher (1539–94): early Arctic explorer
22 The Globe Theatre: William Shakespeare's home base

23 The *Golden Hind*: ship of Sir Francis Drake
24 El Greco (1541–1614): Spanish painter
25 Introduction of the Gregorian calendar, 1582
26 Sir Richard Grenville (1542–91): planted an American colony at Roanoke, Virginia
27 Lady Jane Grey (1537–54): named successor to Edward VI; beheaded
28 Sir Christopher Hatton (1540–91): courtier in Elizabeth's court
29 Sir John Hawkins (1532–95): fought against Spanish Armada
30 Hideyoshi: Japanese military ruler
31 Nicholas Hilliard (1547–1619): famous painter of miniatures
32 Lord Charles Howard: commanded the English fleet against the Armada
33 Thomas Howard, Duke of Norfolk (1536–72): executed for treason

34 Idris Alooma (1571–1603): king of Kanem-Korno, largest trading empire in central Africa

35 Robert Kett: led revolt against enclosure in Norfolk

36 John Knox (1514–72): leader of the Scottish Protestants

37 Bishop Hugh Latimer (1485–1555): martyred at the stake; last words—"We shall this day light such a candle by God's grace in England as, I trust, shall never be put out."

38 Christopher Marlowe (1564–93): dramatist; stabbed in the eye in a pub brawl

39 Mary I (1516–58): called Bloody Mary

40 Mary, Queen of Scots (1542–87): executed by Elizabeth I

41 Gerardus Mercator (1512–94): great Flemish mapmaker

42 Microscopes: invented by Hans and Zacharias Jannsen around 1590

43 Hugh O'Neill, Earl of Tyrone: led a war against the English crown, 1591

44 Robert Parsons (1546–1610): Jesuit plotter against Elizabeth I

45 Philip II of Spain (1527–98): married Bloody Mary

46 Francisco Pizarro (1475–1541): conquered the Incas, 1533

47 Prayer Book Rebellion in Cornwall and Devon: against the rapid religious changes, 1549

48 Sir Walter Raleigh (1554–1618): explorer, poet, scientist, and courtier; put his cloak in a puddle for Elizabeth to cross

49 Gamaliel Ratsey (1578–1605): famous robber

50 Nicholas Ridley (1503–55): Bishop of London; burned at the stake with Hugh Latimer

51 Roanoke colony: vanished, 1590

52 St. Bartholomew's Day Massacre, 1572

53 Sermon of the Plough, 1548: against greedy landowners

54 Edward Seymour, Duke of Somerset: Edward VI's regent; beheaded in 1552

55 William Shakespeare (1564–1616): greatest of the British dramatists

56 Spanish Armada, 1588

57 Edmund Spenser (1552–99): wrote the *Fairie Queene*, dedicated to Elizabeth I

58 Sir Philip Sydney (1554–86): warrior, poet, courtier, and diplomat

59 Thomas Tallis (1505–85): important composer

60 Flush toilet: invented, 1594

61 Sir Francis Walsingham (1532–90): founder of the "Secret Service," which stopped plots against Elizabeth

62 William of Orange: assassinated, 1584

63 St. Francis Xavier (1506–52): missionary in Japan, 1549–51

1 Anne of Denmark: wife of James I
2 The Bellman: a town crier
3 Duke of Buckingham: favorite of Charles I
4 Miguel de Cervantes Saavedra (1547–1616): author of *Don Quixote*
5 Charles I (1600–49): unpopular king; deposed and beheaded
6 René Descartes (1596–1650): father of modern philosophy
7 Robert Devereux, 3rd Earl of Essex (1591–1646): fought the battle of
   Edgehill, 1642

8 John Donne (1572–1631): "metaphysical" poet
9 Sir Thomas Fairfax (1612–71): one of Cromwell's great generals
10 Guy Fawkes (1570–1606): instigator of the Gunpowder Plot, 1605
11 Galileo Galilei (1564–1642): great Italian astronomer
12 Orlando Gibbons (1583–1625): composer
13 William Gilbert (1540–1603): pioneer in the science of electricity
14 Gustavus Adolphus (1594–1632): warlike Swedish king
15 Frans Hals (1581–1666): Dutch painter

16 John Hampden (1594–1643): refused to pay the king's ship tax, 1637
17 Dr. William Harvey (1578–1657): described the circulation of the
   blood
18 Harvard College: first college in America, 1636
19 Sir Ralph Hopton: a popular Royalist general
20 James I (1603–25): first king of "Great Britain"
21 Inigo Jones (1573–1652): great architect
22 Ben Jonson (1572–1637): dramatist

23 King James Bible: 1611
24 William Laud (1573–1645): unpopular archbishop of Canterbury
25 Manchus: overthrew the Ming dynasty to establish the Ching dynasty
26 Peter Minuit (1580–1638): purchased Manhattan from the
   Indians, 1626
27 Monteverdi (1567–1643): inventor of opera
28 Oyo kingdom in Nigeria
29 American Pilgrims, 1620

30 Pocahontas (1595–1617): Powhatan Indian woman who saved the life
   of Captain John Smith, 1608
31 John Pym (1584–1643): politician
32 Rembrandt van Rijn (1606–69): Holland's greatest painter
33 Cardinal Richelieu (1585–1642): power behind the French throne
34 John Rolfe (1585–1622): colonist who married Pocahontas and
   brought her to England
35 Royal Mails: started by Charles I

36 Peter Paul Rubens (1577–1640): Dutch painter who worked in England
37 Prince Rupert (1619–82): Royalist hero of the Battle of Marston Moor
38 Abel Tasman (1603–59): discovered New Zealand and Tasmania, 1642
39 Outbreak of Thirty Years' War
40 Tokugawa Iyeyasu (1543–1616): seized power in Japan and started the
   Shogunate (military dictatorship)
41 Diego Velázquez (1599–1660): Spanish court painter
42 Thomas Wentworth, Earl of Strafford (1593–1641): executed for
   supporting Charles I

1 Adamite: naked member of a religious sect
2 Barebones Parliament: a hand-picked body of Puritans
3 Admiral Robert Blake (1599–1657): defeated the Dutch and made
   England "mistress of the seas"
4 John Bradshaw: president of the court that tried Charles I; wore a
   steel-lined hat for protection

5 Sir Thomas Browne (1605–82): author of *Religio Medici*
6 Charles I (1600–49): beheaded
7 Charles II (1630–1685): hid from assassins in an oak tree
8 Oliver Cromwell (1599–1658): leader of revolution
9 Victims of the Drogheda and Wexford massacres, 1650
10 George Fox (1624–91): founder of the Quakers

11 Thomas Harrison (1606–60): Puritan general
12 Thomas Hobbes (1588–1679): author of *Leviathan*, 1651
13 Lucy Hutchinson: kept a diary of the English Civil War
14 Dutchman Christian Huygens: invented the pendulum clock, 1656
15 General Henry Ireton (1611–51): Cromwell's son-in-law
16 John Lilburne and William Walwyn: political pamphleteers

17 Richard Lovelace (1618–57): "Stone walls do not a prison make / Nor iron bars a cage"

18 Andrew Marvell (1621–78): poet

19 Mazarin (1602–61): the unpopular ruler of France during Louis XIV's childhood

20 John Milton (1608–74): author of *Paradise Lost*

21 Molière (1622–73): French dramatist

22 General George Monk, Duke of Albemarle: commander instrumental in the Restoration of Charles II

23 The Marquess of Ormonde: leader of the Protestant Royalists in Ireland

24 Pepper mill: symbol of the British spice trade

25 Jan Van Riebeck: Dutch explorer (with Hottentot)

26 Rump Parliament: troublesome to Cromwell

27 Taj Mahal: mausoleum in India, built by Shah Jahan

28 Tumbledown Dick: Cromwell's eldest son Richard: soon fell from power

29 Henry Vaughan (1622–95): poet

30 Palace of Whitehall

31 Gerard Winstanley: leader of the "Diggers," who believed in equal rights in property and citizenship

1660

1670

1 Aphra Behn (1690–1789): first English woman to earn a living by writing
2 Thomas Blood (1618–80): better known as Captain Blood—stole the Crown Jewels, 1671
3 Robert Boyle (1627–91): father of modern chemistry
4 John Bunyan (1628–88): author of *Pilgrim's Progress*, 1678
5 Samuel Butler (1612–80): author of *Hudibras*, an anti-Puritan poem
6 Barbara Castlemaine: mistress of Charles II
7 Catherine of Braganza (1638–1705): Charles II's bucktoothed queen

8 Revenge for the death of Charles I: heads on poles
9 Charles II (1630–85): first Restoration king
10 Charles II: had a crane in St. James Park with a wooden leg
11 Seven Bishops: refused to read the *Declaration of Indulgence* in church
12 Dodo bird: extinct by 1680
13 John Dryden (1631–1700): England's poet laureate, 1668–88
14 John Evelyn (1620–1706): founder of the Royal Society
15 Grinling Gibbons: great woodcarver

16 The Great Fire of London, 1666
17 Nell Gwynne (c.1650–87): popular actress and mistress of Charles II
18 Halley's comet
19 Protestant Huguenots exiled from France, 1685
20 Edward Hyde, Earl of Clarendon (1609–74): advisor to Charles II
21 James II (1633–1701): king of England
22 Judge Jeffreys: conducted the Bloody Assizes, 1685
23 Kang Xi (1654–1722): first great Manchu emperor
24 Sieur de La Salle (1643–87): French explorer of the Mississippi

25 Sir Peter Lely (1618–80): portrait painter
26 Louis XIV (1638–1715): "The Sun King" of France
27 Mary of Modena, wife of James II: Baby son smuggled in a warming pan?
28 The Duke of Monmouth (1649–85): illegitimate son of Charles II who claimed the throne in 1685; beheaded
29 Sir Isaac Newton (1642–1727): one of the world's greatest scientific geniuses; formulated the theory of gravity
30 Titus Oates (1649–1705): falsely accused Catholics of plotting against the king, 1678

31 William Penn (1644–1718): founder of Pennsylvania
32 Samuel Pepys (1633–1703): wrote a diary in secret code
33 First pineapple grown in England
34 Plague: the doors of all infected houses were marked with a red cross, 1665
35 Punch and Judy show, 1662
36 Jean Racine (1639–99): French playwright
37 Madame de Sévigné (1626–96): French noblewoman famous for her letters

38 The Earl of Shaftesbury (1621–83): leader of the Cabal (or Inner Council)
39 The Sikhs rose up against Aurangzeb, 1676
40 John III Sobieski: king of Poland, 1629–96
41 Benedict de Spinoza (1632–77): Dutch philosopher
42 Peter Stuyvesant (1610–72): last Dutch governor of New Amsterdam
43 Jan Vermeer (1632–75): Dutch painter
44 Lucy Walter: mistress of Charles II
45 Sir Christopher Wren (1632–1723): great London architect

1 Joseph Addison (1672–1719): author of *The Spectator* essays
2 Queen Anne (1665–1714): a dull monarch, reigned 1702–14
3 George Berkeley (1685–1753): said nothing exists unless perceived by the mind
4 Battle of Blenheim, 1704
5 In Ireland, Battle of the Boyne, 1689

6 Charles XII of Sweden (1682–1718): warlike monarch
7 Sarah Churchill (Jennings): lady-in-waiting to Queen Anne
8 William Congreve (1670–1729): English comic playwright
9 Gabriel Daniel Fahrenheit (1686–1736): German scientist who invented the Fahrenheit temperature scale
10 Celia Fiennes: rode around England on a horse to improve her health

11 George of Denmark: thick and dull; married to Queen Anne
12 The Glencoe Massacre, 1692
13 Sidney Godolphin (1645–1712): First Lord of the Treasury
14 Edmond Halley (1656–1742): English astronomer who predicted the return of the comet named after him
15 Battle of La Hogue: great British naval victory, 1692

16 Anthony van Leeuwenhoek (1632–1723): pioneer microscopist
17 John Locke (1632–1704): English philosopher
18 First Duke of Marlborough (1650–1722): led British to victory in the War of Spanish Succession
19 Queen Mary II (1662–94): daughter of James II; ruled with her husband, William

20 Thomas Newcomen's steam engine, 1712
21 First American newspaper: *The Boston Newsletter*, 1704
22 Battle of Oudenarde, 1708
23 Peter the Great (1672–1725): Europeanized Russia
24 Henry Purcell (1659–95): great English composer
25 Battle of Ramillies, 1706
26 Salem witchcraft trials in New England, 1692

27 Thomas Savery and his steam pump
28 Union Jack: England and Scotland united, 1707
29 Sir John Vanbrugh (1664–1726): architect and playwright
30 Antonio Vivaldi (1678–1741): red-headed Italian composer
31 William III, "William of Orange" (1650–1702): a protestant prince from Holland
32 *The Worcester Journal*, 1690: oldest newspaper in England

1 Caroline Ansbach: wife of George II
2 Thomas Arne: composer of "God Save the King" and "Rule Britannia"
3 Johann Sebastian Bach (1685–1750): great German composer
4 Vitus Bering (1681–1741): Danish explorer
5 Black Hole of Calcutta, 1756
6 Lancelot "Capability" Brown (1716–83): English landscape gardener
7 Admiral George Byng (1663–1733): court-martialed and shot for withdrawing in the face of French fire
8 Canaletto—byname of Giovanni Antonio Canal (1697–1768): famous for his paintings of Venice
9 Bonny Prince Charlie and Flora MacDonald: led the Rebellion of '45

10 Thomas Chippendale, George Hepplewhite, and Thomas Sheraton: famous furniture makers
11 Robert Clive (1725–74): established British power in India
12 Captain Coram: started a foundling home
13 Countess of Darlington: mistress of George I, known as "the Elephant"
14 Daniel Defoe (1660–1731): author of *Robinson Crusoe*
15 Denis Diderot (1713–84): creator of the French encyclopedia
16 Henry Fielding (1707–54): great English comic novelist
17 Benjamin Franklin (1706–90): American founding father, philosopher, and scientist

18 Frederick the Great of Prussia (1712–86): brilliant general, a patron of the arts
19 Frederick, son of George II: hit on the head with a ball and died
20 John Gay (1685–1732): wrote *The Beggar's Opera*
21 George I (1660–1727): always hated England, reigned 1714–27
22 George II (1683–1760): king of England, reigned 1727–60
23 George Frideric Handel (1685–1759): German-born composer; he spent most of his life in England
24 Nicholas Hawksmoor and James Gibbs: architects
25 William Hogarth (1697–1764): English satirical engraver; depicted *Beggar's Opera*

26 David Hume (1711–76): Scottish philosopher
27 Captain Robert Jenkins: cause of the War of Jenkins's Ear, 1739
28 John Kay: invented the "flying shuttle"
29 Duchess of Kendal: George I's German mistress, known as "the Maypole"
30 Jean-Baptiste Lamarck (1744–1829): introduced the term "biology" to describe the study of living things
31 Carl Linnaeus (1707–78): classified plants and animals
32 Louis XV (1710–74): king of France; earned the hatred of his subjects
33 Maria Theresa (1717–80): Habsburg empress
34 Lady Mary Wortley Montagu (1689–1762): spurned Alexander Pope

35 James Oglethorpe (1696–1785): founded Georgia, 1733
36 William Pitt "The Elder" (1708–78): his ideas dominated British government
37 Alexander Pope (1688–1744): poet whose "Rape of the Lock" made him famous
38 Samuel Richardson (1689–1761): early popular novelist
39 Alessandro Scarlatti (1660–1725): Italian composer
40 South Sea Bubble: when the South Sea Company crashed, hundreds went bankrupt
41 Laurence Sterne (1713–68): wrote *Tristram Shandy*
42 Antonio Stradivari (1644–1737): great violin maker

43 James Stuart, the "Old Pretender" (1688–1766): tried to retake the throne in 1715
44 Jonathan Swift (1667–1745): author of *Gulliver's Travels*
45 Viscount "Turnip" Townshend: champion of turnip cultivation
46 Jethro Tull (1674–1741): invented the seed drill
47 Diek Turpin: infamous "highway man"
48 Sir Robert Walpole (1676–1745): Britain's first prime minister
49 Jean-Antoine Watteau (1684–1721): French artist
50 Josiah Wedgwood (1730–95): founder of the famous English pottery
51 John Wesley (1703–91): Founder of the Methodist Church
52 James Wolfe (1727–59): British general who captured Quebec

1 Abigail Adams: wife of President John Adams
2 John Adams (1735–1826): 2nd U.S. president
3 Samuel Adams (1722–1803): American revolutionary
4 Ethan Allen (1738–89): leader of Green Mountain Boys
5 Jeffrey Amherst (1717–97): British general in French and Indian War, 1754–63
6 John André (1750–80): Benedict Arnold's spy partner
7 Benedict Arnold (1741–1801): Revolutionary War turncoat
8 John Jacob Astor (1763–1848): made a fortune in fur
9 Crispus Attucks (1723–70): first casualty of the American Revolution
10 Jane Austen (1775–1817): British novelist
11 William Bainbridge: U.S. naval hero in the War of 1812
12 John and William Bartram: father and son naturalists
13 Ludwig van Beethoven (1770–1827): great German composer
14 William Blake (1757–1827): English visionary poet
15 Blue Jacket: great Indian warrior
16 Daniel Boone (1734–1820): frontiersman
17 James Boswell and Samuel Johnson: biographer and subject

18 Boston Tea Party, 1773
19 Aaron Burr and Alexander Hamilton: duelled, 1804
20 John Burgoyne (1722–92): British general in American Revolution
21 Edmund Burke (1729–97): political philosopher
22 Lord Byron (1788–1824): poet
23 Catherine the Great (1729–96) empress of Russia
24 Toussaint Charbonneau: Sacajawea's husband
25 George Rogers Clark (1752–1818): U.S. frontier general
26 Sir Henry Clinton (1738–95): British general in American Revolution
27 John Colter: American mountain man
28 Captain James Cook (1728–79): explored Hawaii
29 John Singleton Copley (1738–1815): early American painter
30 Charlotte Corday (1768–93): stabbed Jean-Paul Marat
31 Cornplanter: 18th-century Indian leader
32 Georges Danton (1759–94): leader in French Revolution
33 Stephen Decatur (1779–1820): naval hero of war of 1812
34 John Forbes: British general in French and Indian War, 1754–63
35 Benjamin Franklin (1706–90): kite-flying founding father

36 Robert Fulton (1765–1815): *Clermont* steamboat, 1807
37 Thomas Gage (1721–87): British general in American Revolution
38 Edmond Genêt (1763–1834): XYZ Affair, 1798
39 George III (1738–1820): British king during American Revolution
40 Hugh Glass: mountain man
41 Johann Wolfgang von Goethe (1749–1832): German literary genius
42 Francisco de Goya (1746–1828): Spanish painter
43 Guillotine: fixture of the French Revolution
44 Nathan Hale (1755–76): martyred spy of the U.S. Revolution
45 Wade Hampton (1751–1835): American Revolutionary general
46 John Hancock (1737–93): first signer of the *Declaration of Independence*
47 William Howe (1729–1814): British general in American Revolution
48 Washington Irving (1783–1859): first great American writer
49 Andrew Jackson (1767–1845): 7th U.S. president
50 John Jay (1745–1829): 1st Supreme Court chief justice
51 Thomas Jefferson (1743–1826): 3rd U.S. president
52 John Paul Jones (1747–92): U.S. naval hero of the Revolution

53 Empress Josephine (1763–1814): wife of Napoleon I
54 Simon Kenton: American mountain man
55 Francis Scott Key (1779–1843): wrote "The Star-Spangled Banner," 1814
56 Jean Lafitte: pirate ally of Andrew Jackson
57 Marquis de Lafayette (1757–1834): French hero of the American Revolution
58 Benjamin Latrobe (1764–1820): completed U.S. Capitol
59 Lighthorse Harry Lee (1756–1818): American revolutionary general
60 Meriwether Lewis and William Clark: great expedition of 1804
61 Manuel Lisa: American fur trader
62 Little Turtle: defeated U.S. Army, 1791
63 Dolley Madison (1768–1849): wife of President Madison
64 James Madison (1751–1836): 4th U.S. president
65 Marie Antoinette (1755–93): wife of Louis XVI; beheaded
66 John Marshall (1755–1835): great Supreme Court chief justice
67 Charles Mason and Jeremiah Dixon: surveyed the Mason-Dixon line
68 James Monroe (1758–1831): 5th U.S. president
69 Marquis de Montcalm (1712–59): French general who lost Quebec
70 Daniel Morgan (1736–1802): American revolutionary general

71 Robert Morris (1734–1806): helped finance the American Revolution
72 Wolfgang Amadeus Mozart (1756–91): great Austrian composer
73 Napoléon I (1769–1821): conqueror of Europe
74 Retreat from Moscow: Napoleon's 1812 defeat
75 Admiral Horatio Nelson (1758–1805): victor over Napoleon's navy
76 Lord North (1732–92): British prime minister during American Revolution
77 James Otis (1725–83): U.S. revolutionary statesman
78 Thomas Paine (1737–1809): wrote *Common Sense*, 1776
79 Oliver Hazard Perry (1785–1819): hero of Lake Erie, 1813
80 Molly Pitcher: heroine of the American Revolution
81 Madame Pompadour (1721–64): mistress to Louis XV
82 Assassination of Chief Pontiac, 1769
83 Israel Putnam (1718–90): American Revolutionary general
84 Paul Revere (1735–1818): alerted the Minutemen, 1775
85 Maximilien-François Robespierre (1758–94): French Revolutionary leader
86 Robert Rogers (1731–95): his Rangers fought on the frontier
87 Sacajawea: Indian woman who helped Lewis and Clark

88 Arthur St. Clair: army was beaten by Little Turtle, 1791
89 Earl of Sandwich: invented the sandwich
90 Junipero Serra (1713–84): Spanish missionary-explorer
91 Shaka the Great: Zulu warrior leader
92 Daniel Shays (1747–1825): led Shays' Rebellion, 1786–87
93 Tecumseh (1768–1813): Shawnee leader in War of 1812
94 Toussaint L'Ouverture: liberator of Haiti
95 Charles Townshend: author of the Townshend Acts
96 Voltaire (1694–1778): French thinker
97 Artemus Ward (1727–1800): U.S. revolutionary general
98 George Washington (1732–99): first U.S. president
99 Martha Washington: wife of the first U.S. president
100 James Watt (1736–1819): first practical steam engine, 1765
101 Duke of Wellington (1769–1852): beat Napoleon at Waterloo, 1815
102 Benjamin West (1738–1820): early American history painter
103 Eli Whitney (1765–1825): invented the cotton gin
104 Whiskey Rebellion: civil disorder in 1794
105 William Wordsworth (1770–1850): great English poet

1 John Quincy Adams (1767–1848): 6th U.S. president
2 Louis Agassiz (1807–73): scientist
3 Hans Christian Andersen (1805–75): Danish spinner of tales
4 Susan B. Anthony (1820–1906): feminist
5 Jesse Applegate: western trailblazer
6 John James Audubon (1785–1851): painter of birds
7 Moses Austin (1767–1821): founder of Texas colony
8 Stephen F. Austin (1793–1836): early Texas leader
9 Honoré de Balzac (1799–1850): French novelist
10 Jim Beckwourth: African-American mountain man
11 Catherine Beecher: feminist daughter of Henry
12 Henry Ward Beecher (1813–87): popular preacher, abolitionist
13 James Gordon Bennett (1795–1872): newspaper tycoon
14 St. Bernadette (1844–79): had vision of the Virgin Mary
15 Black Hawk (1767–1838): Sac and Fox Indian leader
16 Simón Bolívar (1783–1830): liberator of Bolivia
17 Gail Borden (1801–74): founded a food empire
18 Jim Bowie (1796–1836): defender of the Alamo
19 Louis Braille (1809–52): invented a way for the blind to read
20 James Bridger (1804–81): mountain man

21 The Brontës (Charlotte, Emily, and Anne): novelists
22 John Brown (1800–59): abolitionist
23 James Buchanan (1791–1868): 15th U.S. president
24 John C. Calhoun (1782–1850): champion of Southern "state rights"
25 Kit Carson (1809–68): western trailblazer
26 Thomas Carlyle (1795–1881): British social critic and historian
27 Jesse Chisholm: western cattle baron
28 Frédéric Chopin (1810–49): Polish-French composer
29 Edwin Christy: leader of the Christy Minstrels, mid-1800s
30 Henry Clay (1777–1852): compromise delayed Civil War
31 De Witt Clinton (1769–1828): started the Erie Canal
32 Samuel Colt: six-shooter maker
33 James Fenimore Cooper (1789–1851): frontier novelist
34 Peter Cooper (1791–1883): educator of the working man
35 Davy Crockett (1786–1836): frontiersman and defender of the Alamo
36 Louis Daguerre (1789–1851): inventor of photography
37 Charles Darwin (1809–82): theory of evolution
38 John Deere (1804–86): invented steel plow, 1836
39 Charles Dickens (1812–70): beloved English novelist
40 Emily Dickinson (1830–86): eccentric American poet

41 Stephen Douglas (1813–61): debated Lincoln before the Civil War
42 Frederick Douglass (1817–95): ex-slave, freedom fighter
43 Edwin L. Drake: struck oil in Pennsylvania, 1859
44 Alexandre Dumas, père (1802–70): romantic adventure novelist
45 George Eliot (1819–80): British realistic novelist—a woman
46 Ralph Waldo Emerson (1803–82): American philosopher
47 William George Fargo (1818–81): Western freight man
48 Millard Fillmore (1800–74): 13th U.S. president
49 Stephen Foster (1826–64): songwriter
50 John Frémont (1813–90): intrepid California explorer
51 Margaret Fuller (1810–50): "Transcendental" philosopher
52 George IV (1762–1830): king of England
53 Nikolay Gogol (1809–52): Russian novelist
54 Charles Goodyear (1800–60): invented vulcanization of rubber, 1839
55 Asa Gray (1810–88): naturalist
56 Horace Greeley (1811–72): "Go West, young man!"
57 Grimm, Jacob (1785–1863) and Wilhelm (1786–1859): collected folk tales
58 William Henry Harrison (1773–1841): 9th U.S. president
59 Bret Harte (1836–1902): western writer
60 Nathaniel Hawthorne (1804–64): wrote The Scarlet Letter, 1850

61 Heinrich Heine (1797–1856): German poet
62 Ben Holladay: western freight man
63 Oliver Wendell Holmes, Sr. (1809–94): poet and physician
64 Sam Houston (1793–1863): hero of Texas War of Independence
65 John Keats (1795–1821): short-lived English Romantic poet
66 Franz Liszt (1811–86): Hungarian composer
67 Henry Wadsworth Longfellow (1807–82): author of *Hiawatha*, 1855
68 James Russell Lowell (1819–91): popular poet
69 Horace Mann (1796–1859): champion of public education
70 James Marshall: discovered gold at Sutter's Mill, 1848
71 Karl Marx (1818–83): father of Communism
72 Cyrus McCormick (1809–84): invented reaper, 1834
73 Ben McCullough: legendary Texas Ranger
74 William Holmes McGuffey (1800–73): taught generations to read
75 Herman Melville (1819–91): wrote *Moby Dick*, 1851
76 Lola Montez (1818–61): sensational entertainer in the West
77 Moroni: Mormon angel
78 Samuel Morse (1791–1872): invented the telegraph, 1844
79 Florence Nightingale (1820–1910): great nurse and reformer of health care
80 Frederick Law Olmsted (1822–1903): designed New York's Central Park

81 Osceola (1800–38): leader of the Seminoles
82 Niccolò Paganini (1782–1840): great violinist
83 Louis Pasteur (1822–95): microbe hunter
84 Matthew Perry (1794–1858): opened relations between the U.S. and Japan
85 Franklin Pierce (1804–69): 14th U.S. president
86 Zebulon Pike (1779–1813): early explorer of the Far West
87 Edgar Allan Poe (1809–49): horror writer
88 James Knox Polk (1795–1849): 11th U.S. president
89 Antonio López de Santa Anna (1794–1876): lost the Mexican War, 1846–48
90 George Sand (1804–76): French novelist—a woman
91 Dred Scott (1795–1858): slave the Supreme Court didn't free, 1857
92 Winfield Scott (1786–1866): hero of the Mexican War, 1846–48
93 Sequoyah (1760–1843): invented the Cherokee alphabet
94 Singer and Howe: Sewing machine rivals
95 Pierre de Smet: Catholic missionary in the West
96 Joseph Smith, Jr. (1805–44): founder of Mormonism
97 Sojourner Truth (1797–1883): ex-slave, freedom fighter
98 Elizabeth Cady Stanton (1815–1902): suffragist and abolitionist
99 Harriet Beecher Stowe (1811–96): wrote *Uncle Tom's Cabin*, 1852
100 Johann Strauss, Father (1804–49) and Son (1825–99): waltz kings

101 Charles Sumner (1811–74): caned on the floor of the Senate
102 Roger Taney (1777–1864): judge in the Dred Scott case, 1857
103 Zachary Taylor (1784–1850): 12th U.S. president
104 Henry David Thoreau (1817–62): wrote *Walden*, 1854
105 William B. Travis: defender of the Alamo
106 Harriet Tubman and Wendell Phillips: abolitionists
107 Nat Turner (1800–31): led violent slave rebellion, 1831
108 John Tyler (1790–1862): 10th U.S. president
109 Underground Railroad: road to freedom for runaway slaves
110 Martin Van Buren (1782–1862): 8th U.S. president
111 Giuseppe Verdi (1813–1901): great Italian opera composer
112 Queen Victoria (1819–1901): ruler of the British Empire at its height
113 Conte Alessandro Volta (1745–1827): experimenter with electricity
114 Richard Wagner (1813–83): German opera titan
115 Daniel Webster vs. Robert Hayne: slavery debate
116 Noah Webster (1758–1843): author of an *American Dictionary*, 1783
117 John Greenleaf Whittier (1807–92): poet
118 Walt Whitman (1819–92): wrote *Leaves of Grass*, 1855
119 Brigham Young (1801–77): led the Mormon Trek, 1847–48

1 Louisa May Alcott (1832–88): author of *Little Women*
2 American Horse: Sioux chief
3 Chester A. Arthur (1829–86): 21st U.S. president
4 Frédéric-Auguste Bartholdi: created the Statue of Liberty, 1880
5 Clara Barton (1821–1912): founded the American Red Cross
6 Sam Bass: western bandit
7 Judge Roy Bean: "Law West of the Pecos"
8 P. G. T. Beauregard (1818–93): Confederate general
9 Alexander Graham Bell (1847–1922): invented the telephone, 1876
10 Frederick Benteen: survivor of the Little Bighorn, 1876
11 Ambrose Bierce (1842–1914): Civil War writer
12 Billy the Kid: legendary western badman
13 Otto von Bismarck (1815–98): unified Germany
14 Black Bart: infamous western stagecoach robber
15 Edwin Booth (1833–93): greatest actor of his age
16 John Wilkes Booth (1838–65): assassinated Lincoln, 1865
17 Mathew Brady (1823–96): Civil War photographer
18 Johannes Brahms (1833–97): great German composer
19 William Jennings Bryan (1860–1925): orator

20 Buffalo Bill (1846–1917): master of the Wild West Show
21 Ambrose Burnside (1824–81): Union general with "sideburns"
22 Joseph Campbell (d. 1900): canned soup king
23 Andrew Carnegie (1835–1919): philanthropist
24 Lewis Carroll (1832–98): wrote *Alice in Wonderland*
25 Carpetbaggers: post–Civil War scoundrels
26 Butch Cassidy and the Sundance Kid: Hole-in-the-Wall Gang
27 Mary Cassatt (1845–1926): painter
28 Clanton clan: fought at the O.K. Corral against the Earps, 1881
29 Grover Cleveland (1837–1908): 22nd and 24th U.S. president
30 Cochise (1812–74): great Apache warrior
31 Crazy Horse (1849–77): defeated Custer
32 George Armstrong Custer (1839–76): Last Stand, 1871
33 Jefferson Davis (1808–89): Confederate president
34 Claude Debussy (1862–1918): French composer
35 George Dewey (1837–1917): admiral hero of Spanish-American War
36 Benjamin Disraeli (1804–81): Queen Victoria's prime minister
37 Dorothea Dix (1802–87): Civil War social reformer
38 Grenville Dodge: builder of the Union Pacific

39 Thomas Eakins (1844–1916): realist painter
40 Jubal Early (1816–94): Confederate general
41 Earp brothers: legendary Tombstone, Arizona, lawmen/gunmen
42 Thomas Alva Edison (1847–1931): invented incandescent electric light
43 Eiffel Tower: Paris landmark
44 William Farragut: Union naval commander
45 Marshall Field (1834–1906): department store pioneer
46 James Garfield (1831–81): 20th U.S. president; assassinated
47 Giuseppe Garibaldi (1807–82): Italian freedom fighter
48 Geronimo (1829–1909): Apache leader in the Southwest
49 King Gillette (1855–1932): inventor of the safety razor
50 William Gladstone (1809–98): successor to Disraeli
51 Golden Spike: joined the Central and Union Pacific railroads
52 Ulysses S. Grant (1822–85): Union general-in-chief, 18th U.S. president
53 Charles Guiteau: President Garfield's assassin, 1881
54 Benjamin Harrison (1833–1901): 23rd U.S. president
55 Rutherford B. Hayes (1822–93): 19th U.S. president
56 William Randolph Hearst (1863–1951): newspaper tycoon
57 Wild Bill Hickok (1837–76): legendary western lawman and gambler

58 Doc Holliday: desperate dentist and friend of the Earps
59 Winslow Homer (1836–1910): artist
60 Fighting Joe Hooker (1814–79): Union general
61 Gerard Manley Hopkins (1844–89): British poet
62 Julia Ward Howe (1819–1910): author of "Battle Hymn of the Republic"
63 Victor Hugo (1802–85): wrote *Hunchback of Notre Dame*
64 Impressionist painters
65 Stonewall Jackson (1824–63): Confederate general
66 Frank and Jesse James: infamous badman brothers of the West
67 Andrew Johnson (1808–75): unpopular 17th U.S. president
68 A. S. Johnston (1803–62): Confederate general
69 Joseph Johnston (1807–91): Confederate general
70 Scott Joplin (1868–1917): ragtime master
71 Theodore Dehone Judah: mastermind of the Union Pacific
72 William and John Kellogg: cereal creators
73 James King: owner of one of the greatest of all Texas ranches
74 Ku Klux Klansmen: hooded bigots
75 Robert E. Lee (1807–70): Confederate general-in-chief
76 Abraham Lincoln (1809–65) 16th U.S. president: Civil War leader
77 Mary Todd Lincoln: wife of Abraham

78 David Livingstone (1813–73): lost in Africa; found by Henry Stanley
79 George McClellan (1826–85): Union general
80 George Meade (1815–72): Union hero of Gettysburg
81 J. P. Morgan, Sr. (1837–1913): financier
82 John Muir (1838–1914): founded the Sierra Club
83 Thomas Nast (1840–1902): satirical cartoonist
84 Carrie Nation (1846–1911): smasher of saloons
85 Alfred Nobel (1833–96): created dynamite and the Nobel Prize
86 Annie Oakley (1860–1926): celebrated markswoman
87 Mrs. O'Leary: her cow started the Chicago Fire, 1871
88 John S. Pemberton (1831–88): inventor of Coca-Cola
89 George Pickett (1825–75): Confederate general
90 Allan J. Pinkerton (1819–84): first private eye
91 Pony Express: first Express Mail
92 Giacomo Puccini (1858–1924): composer of beautiful operas
93 Joseph Pulitzer (1847–1911): newspaper tycoon
94 Red Cloud (1822–1909): Sioux war leader
95 John Rockefeller (1839–1937): founded Standard Oil, 1870
96 Auguste Rodin (1840–1917): French sculptor of *The Thinker*
97 Sears and Roebuck: founders of the catalog business

98 William Seward (1801–72): U.S. secretary of state who bought Alaska
99 George Bernard Shaw (1856–1950): British playwright
100 Philip Sheridan (1831–88): Civil War general and Indian fighter
101 William Tecumseh Sherman (1820–91): Union general
102 Sitting Bull (1831–90): Hunkpapa Sioux leader
103 Leland Stanford: financier of the Union Pacific
104 John Stetson: cowboys' hatter
105 Robert Louis Stevenson (1850–94): author of *Kidnapped*
106 J. E. B. Stuart (1833–64): Confederate general
107 John L. Sullivan (1858–1918): great boxer defeated by Jim Corbett
108 Billy Sunday (1862–1935): revivalist preacher
109 Pyotr Ilich Tchaikovsky (1840–93): Russian composer
110 Leo Tolstoy (1828–1910): wrote *War and Peace*
111 Henri de Toulouse-Lautrec (1864–1901): French, short-legged painter
112 Mark Twain (1835–1910): beloved American writer
113 Jules Verne (1828–1905): French author, inventor of sci fi
114 Booker T. Washington (1856–1915): educator
115 James Abbott McNeill Whistler: painter, *Whistler's Mother*, 1871–72
116 Frank W. Woolworth (1852–1919): started the 5 & 10 chain, 1879
117 Émile Zola (1840–1902): crusading French writer

1 Roald Amundsen (1872–1928): first to reach South Pole, 1911
2 Louis Armstrong (1901–71): jazz trumpeter
3 Fred Astaire (1899–1987): film's greatest dancer
4 Kemal Ataturk: father of modern Turkey, 1923
5 Josephine Baker (1906–75): African-American entertainer
6 Irving Berlin and Jerome Kern: great popular songwriters
7 Sarah Bernhardt (1844–1923): great actress
8 Clarence Birdseye: invented frozen food, 1920s
9 Bonnie and Clyde: 1930s crime couple
10 James Cagney: tough guy actor of the 1930s
11 Al Capone (1899–1947): crime kingpin
12 Enrico Caruso (1873–1921): great Italian tenor
13 Coco Chanel (1883–1971): fashion designer
14 Charlie Chaplin (1889–1977): "Little Tramp" film star
15 Georges Clemenceau (1841–1929): WW I French leader
16 Mad Dog Coll: infamous 1920s gangster
17 Calvin Coolidge (1872–1933): 30th U.S. president
18 Marie and Pierre Curie: discovered radium, 1898

19 Leon Czolgosz: assassinated President McKinley, 1901
20 Salvador Dalí (1904–89): surrealist painter
21 Jack Dempsey: heavyweight boxing champ, 1927
22 John Dillinger: Public Enemy No. 1, 1934
23 Isadora Duncan (1877–1927): unconventional dancer
24 Amelia Earhart: aviator who disappeared in 1937
25 Albert Einstein (1879–1955): physicist, Theory of Relativity, 1905
26 Duke Ellington (1899–1974): jazz composer and band leader
27 Douglas Fairbanks, Sr. and Mary Pickford: famous movie couple
28 W. C. Fields (1880–1946): film funny man
29 F. Scott and Zelda Fitzgerald: Jazz-age author and wife
30 Henry Ford (1863–1947): invented automobile Model T, 1908
31 Sigmund Freud (1856–1939): founded psychoanalysis
32 Clark Gable (1901–60): male lead in *Gone With The Wind*, 1939
33 Mohandas Gandhi (1869–1948): India's champion of independence
34 Greta Garbo (1905–90): film goddess
35 Marcus Garvey (1887–1940): radical black leader
36 George Gershwin (1898–1937): jazz composer

37 Amadeo Giannini: founded Bank of America, 1904
38 Warren G. Harding (1865–1923): 29th U.S. president
39 Ernest Hemingway (1899–1961): great novelist
40 Emperor Hirohito (1901–89): Japanese emperor, 1926–89
41 Herbert Hoover (1874–1964): 31st U.S. president
42 J. Edgar Hoover (1895–1972): FBI director
43 Hoover and Spangler: inventors of the vacuum cleaner
44 Harry Houdini (1874–1926): escape artist
45 Edwin Hubble (1889–1953): astronomy pioneer
46 Howard Hughes (1905–76): eccentric tycoon
47 Shoeless Joe Jackson: cheated in the World Series of 1919
48 Jack Johnson: heavyweight boxing champ, 1908
49 Bobby Jones (1902–71): golf legend
50 Casey Jones: heroic train engineer
51 Mother Jones (1830–1930): labor leader
52 Franz Kafka (1883–1924): Austrian, surrealist writer
53 Buster Keaton (1895–1966): comic star of silent film
54 Helen Keller (1880–1968): blind and deaf lecturer

55 Laurel and Hardy: comic movie actors, 1920s
56 Ernest Lawrence (1901–58): atomic physicist
57 Vivien Leigh (1913–67): female lead in *Gone With The Wind*, 1939
58 V. I. Lenin (1870–1924): leader of the Bolshevik Revolution, 1917
59 Charles A. Lindbergh (1902–74): flew solo across the Atlantic, 1927
60 David Lloyd George (1863–1945): WW I British prime minister
61 Joe Louis: heavyweight boxing champ, 1937
62 Lucky Luciano (1897–1962): crime kingpin
63 *Lusitania*: torpedoed 1916
64 Follower of Mao Tse-tung on the "Great March"
65 Guglielmo Marconi (1874–1937): invented radio, 1901
66 Groucho Marx: Marx Brothers movies, 1930s
67 William McKinley (1843–1901): 25th U.S. president; assassinated
68 Mickey Mouse: host of Walt Disney World
69 Eliot Ness: crimefighter, 1930s
70 Nicholas II and Alexandra: last Russian czar and czarina
71 Frank Nitty: criminal kingpin, foe of Eliot Ness
72 Georgia O'Keeffe (1887–1986): great modern painter

73 Vittorio Orlando (1860–1952): Italian prime minister
74 Jesse Owens: Olympic victor in Munich, 1936
75 Ivan Pavlov (1849–1936): dogs proved his psychological theory
76 Robert Peary and Matthew Henson: reached North Pole, 1909
77 John Pershing (1860–1948): U.S. commander, WW I
78 Edith Piaf (1915–63): French singer
79 Pablo Picasso (1881–1973): reshaped modern art
80 Cole Porter (1891–1964): witty songwriter
81 Jeanette Rankin: first Congresswoman, 1916
82 Rasputin (1872–1916): "Mad Monk" advisor to Czar Nicholas II and wife
83 John Reed (1887–1920): U.S. historian of Russian Revolution, 1919
84 Eddie Rickenbacker (1890–1973): U.S. WW I air ace, 1918
85 Norman Rockwell (1894–1978): America's favorite illustrator
86 Ginger Rogers (1911–95): Fred Astaire's dancing partner
87 Will Rogers (1879–1935): cowboy comic
88 Theodore Roosevelt (1858–1919): 26th U.S. president
89 Babe Ruth (1895–1948): baseball legend
90 San Francisco earthquake, 1906

91 Margaret Sanger (1883–1966): birth control pioneer
92 Upton Sinclair (1878–1968): wrote *The Jungle*, 1906
93 Superman: aka Clark Kent
94 William Howard Taft (1857–1930): 27th U.S. president
95 Shirley Temple: child star of the 1930s
96 Jim Thorpe (1866–1953): Native American Olympic victor, 1912
97 Bill Tilden (1893–1953): tennis great
98 Rudolph Valentino (1895–1926): silent screen legend
99 Pancho Villa (1878–1923): Mexican revolutionary
100 Kaiser Wilhelm II: WW I German ruler
101 Woodrow Wilson (1856–1924): 28th U.S. president
102 Winnie the Pooh: favorite storybook character created by A. A. Milne
103 *Wizard of Oz*: written in 1900 by Frank Baum
104 Frank Lloyd Wright (1867–1959): great architect
105 Wilbur and Orville Wright: invented the airplane, 1903
106 Sergeant Alvin York (1887–1964): U.S. WW I hero
107 Florenz Ziegfeld (1869–1932): great showman
108 Vladimir Zworykin: invented "iconoscope" (TV), 1933

1 James Baldwin (1924–87): African-American writer
2 Lucille Ball (1911–89): great comedienne
3 Jack Benny (1894–1974): radio and TV comic
4 Leonard Bernstein (1918–90): great conductor-composer
5 Milton Berle: TV's "Uncle Miltie" of the 1950s
6 Berlin Airlift, 1948
7 Chuck Berry: duck-walking rock 'n' roller
8 Humphrey Bogart and Ingrid Bergman: costarred in *Casablanca*, 1943
9 Margaret Bourke-White (1906–71): photojournalist
10 Marlon Brando: new generation of American film actor
11 Ralph Bunche (1904–71): African-American U.S. ambassador to the U.N.
12 Fidel Castro: Cuban dictator since 1959
13 Neville Chamberlain: made a worthless peace pact with Hitler, 1938
14 Whitaker Chambers: accused Alger Hiss of spying, 1950
15 Sir Winston Churchill (1874–1965): Britain's WW II leader
16 Patsy Cline: "I Fall to Pieces" country singer
17 Nat King Cole: smooth singer of the 1950s

18 Francis Crick and James Watson: discovered DNA, 1953
19 Dalai Lama: leader of Tibetan Buddhism
20 Miles Davis (1926–91): "Cool" trumpet player
21 James Dean: young film idol killed in a car crash, 1955
22 Cecil B. DeMille (1881–1951): epic director
23 Joe DiMaggio: baseball great
24 John Foster Dulles (1888–1959): U.S. secretary of state
25 Edward VIII (1894–1972): left the throne for love, 1936
26 Dwight D. Eisenhower (1890–1969): WW II supreme allied commander and 34th U.S. president
27 William Faulkner (1897–1962): Nobel Prize–winning novelist
28 Enrico Fermi (1901–54): nuclear reactor scientist
29 Ella Fitzgerald: "first lady" of jazz song
30 Francisco Franco (1892–1975): Spain's dictator, 1936–75
31 Anne Frank: wrote a Holocaust diary
32 Dizzy Gillespie (1917–93): Bebop trumpeter
33 Allen Ginsberg: king of the "Beat" poets, 1950s

34 Joseph Goebbels (1897–1945): Hitler henchman
35 Hermann Goering (1893–1946): Hitler henchman
36 Betty Grable: most famous legs of the 1940s
37 Che Guevara (1928–67): Castro's revolutionary ally
38 Bill Haley and the Comets: "Rock Around the Clock"
39 Rudolf Hess (1894–1987): Hitler henchman
40 Sir Edmund Hillary and Tenzing Norkay: climbed Mt. Everest, 1953
41 Heinrich Himmler (1900–45): Hitler henchman
42 Sir Alfred Hitchcock (1899–1980): director of suspense films
43 Adolf Hitler (1889–1945): Nazi dictator, 1933–45
44 Ho Chi Minh (1890–1969): North Vietnam's communist leader
45 Bob Hope: popular comic
46 Charles Ives (1874–1954): ultramodern composer
47 Grace Kelly and Prince Ranier: fairy-tale wedding, 1956
48 Kermit the Frog: Muppet
49 Jack Kerouac (1922–69): wrote *On the Road*
50 Nikita Khrushchev (1894–1971): shoe-pounding leader of U.S.S.R, 1958–64

51 Ray Kroc (1902–84): McDonald's founder
52 Fiorello La Guardia (1882–1947): New York mayor, 1933–45
53 Edwin Land: invented Polaroid camera, 1947
54 Jerry Lee Lewis: rock 'n' roll wild man
55 Little Richard: rock 'n' roller
56 Douglas MacArthur (1880–1964): U.S. WW II general
57 Mao Tse-tung (1893–1976): leader of Chinese communism
58 George Marshall (1880–1959): aided Europe
59 Willy Mays: baseball great of the 1950s
60 Joseph McCarthy and Roy Cohn: anti-communist "witch hunters"
61 Arthur Miller (b. 1915): playwright
62 Glenn Miller (1904–44): trombonist and band leader
63 Thelonious Monk (1917–82): Bebop pianist
64 Marilyn Monroe (1926–62): stunning screen actress
65 Bernard Law Montgomery (1887–1976): WW II British commander
66 Grandma Moses (1860–1961): senior citizen painter
67 Audie Murphy: WW II hero and movie star

68 Benito Mussolini (1883–1945): Italian dictator, 1922–45
69 Chester A. Nimitz (1885–1966): American WW II admiral
70 J. Robert Oppenheimer (1904–67): atom bomb maker
71 Satchel Paige: great African-American baseball player
72 Charlie Parker: Bebop saxophonist
73 Dorothy Parker (1893–1967): witty writer and critic
74 Rosa Parks: Montgomery civil rights bus boycott, 1955
75 George S. Patton (1885–1945): "blood and guts" U.S. WW II general
76 Eva Peron: Argentina's "Evita"—dictator's wife
77 Jackson Pollock (1912–56): abstract "drip" painter
78 Vidkun Quisling: sold out Norway to the Nazis
79 Paul Robeson (1898–1976): African-American singer
80 Jackie Robinson: first African-American in the major leagues, 1947
81 Erwin Rommel (1891–1944): Nazis' "Desert Fox"
82 Eleanor Roosevelt (1884–1962): humanitarian wife of FDR
83 Franklin D. Roosevelt (1882–1945): 32nd U.S. president
84 Julius and Ethel Rosenberg: executed for treason, 1953

85 J. D. Salinger: author of Catcher in the Rye, 1951
86 Jonas Salk: developed polio vaccine, 1955
87 Igor Sikorsky (1889–1972): invented helicopter, 1939
88 Wallis Simpson: Edward VIII's beloved
89 Frank Sinatra: singer with trademark hat
90 Dr. Benjamin Spock: baby expert
91 Josef Stalin (1879–1953): Soviet dictator, 1924–53
92 Ed Sullivan: popular TV variety host
93 Edward Teller: father of the H-bomb, 1950s
94 Harry S. Truman (1884–1972): 33rd U.S. president
95 Raoul Wallenberg (1912–47): helped Jews escape from Nazis
96 John Wayne (1907–79): macho film star
97 Orson Welles (1915–85): director/star of Citizen Kane
98 Hank Williams (1923–53): country music great
99 Tennessee Williams (1911–83): playwright
100 Chuck Yeager: broke the sound barrier, 1947
101 Georgy K. Zhukov (1896–1974): WW II Soviet commander

1 Hank Aaron (1934–): broke Babe Ruth's home run record, 1974
2 Buzz Aldrin (1930–): 2nd astronaut to land on the moon
3 Muhammad Ali (1942–): boxing great, 1960s and 1970s
4 Yasser Arafat: leader of the PLO
5 Neil Armstrong (1930–): first astronaut to land on the moon, 1969
6 Arthur Ashe (1943–93): African-American tennis great
7 Jim Bakker: TV evangelist who fell from grace
8 Barney the Dinosaur: kids' purple favorite
9 Menachem Begin (1913–92): Israeli prime minister who made peace with Egypt
10 Ivan Boesky: Wall Street raider of the 1980s
11 Wernher von Braun (1912–77): German-born American rocket scientist
12 Barbara Bush: wife of President George Bush
13 George Bush (1924–): 41st U.S. president
14 William Calley: tried for the My Lai Massacre during the Vietnam War, 1968
15 Truman Capote (1924–84): author of *In Cold Blood*, 1966
16 Johnny Carson: most popular TV talk show host
17 Rachel Carson (1907–64): environmentalist author of *Silent Spring*, 1962

18 Jimmy Carter (1924–): 39th U.S. president
19 Charles, Prince of Wales (1948–): fairy-tale marriage to Princess Di dissolved
20 Charlie Brown: lead character of *Peanuts* comic strip
21 Cher: popular singer and actress
22 Barney Clark: received first artificial heart, 1982
23 Bill Clinton (1946–): 42nd U.S. president
24 Hillary Clinton: wife of Bill Clinton
25 Michael Collins (1930–): astronaut
26 Kevin Costner: movie idol of the 1980s and 1990s
27 Robert Crippen and John Young: first space shuttle mission, 1981
28 Walt Disney (1901–66): creator of Mickey Mouse
29 Bob Dylan (1941–): folk-rock singer
30 Mama Cass Eliot: rotund member of The Mamas and the Papas
31 Bobby Fischer (1943–): eccentric chess champion
32 Gerald Ford (1913–): 38th U.S. president
33 Harrison Ford: the movies' Indiana Jones
34 Fred Flintstone: head of cartoon's "modern stone-age family"
35 Betty Friedan (1921–): author of *The Feminine Mystique*, 1963

36 Mu'ammar Gadhafi (1942–): terrorist ruler of Libya
37 Yury Gagarin (1934–68): Russian cosmonaut and first man in space
38 Bill Gates (1955–): software pioneer and richest man in America
39 John Glenn (1921–): first U.S. astronaut to orbit earth, 1962
40 Mikhail Gorbachev (1931–): last general secretary of the Soviet Communist Party, 1985–91
41 Ham: first U.S. chimpanzee in space
42 Patty Hearst: newspaper heiress-turned-radical, 1974
43 Jimi Hendrix: short-lived master of the electric guitar
44 Abbie Hoffman: 1960s "Yippie" radical
45 Jesse Jackson (1941–): civil rights activist
46 Michael Jackson: rock icon of the 1980s
47 Pope John Paul II (1920–): Polish political activist who became Pope in 1978
48 Lady Bird Johnson: wife of LBJ
49 Lyndon B. Johnson (1908–73): 36th U.S. president
50 Magic Johnson: basketball star of the 1980s
51 Janis Joplin: short-lived queen of rock 'n' roll
52 Michael Jordan: basketball great of the 1980s and 1990s

53 Jaqueline Kennedy: elegant wife of JFK
54 John Fitzgerald Kennedy (1917–63): 35th U.S. president; assassinated
55 Robert Kennedy (1925–68): Attorney General, brother of JFK; assassinated
56 Ayatollah Khomeini (1900–89): terrorist leader of Iran
57 Billie Jean King (1943–): women's tennis great
58 Martin Luther King, Jr. (1929–68): civil rights leader; assassinated
59 Rodney King: victim of police beating; sparked Los Angeles riots, 1991
60 Henry Kissinger (1923–): President Nixon's secretary of state
61 John Lennon: Beatles member; assassinated, 1980
62 Roy Lichtenstein: prominent "Pop" artist of the 1960s
63 Madonna: glitzy goddess of 1980s rock
64 John Major (1943–): elected prime minister of Great Britain, 1990
65 Malcolm X (1925–65): radical black activist
66 Nelson Mandela (1918–): from South African political prisoner to president, 1994
67 Christa McAuliffe: schoolteacher-astronaut killed in *Challenger* shuttle disaster, 1986
68 Eugene McCarthy (1916–): liberal presidential candidate, 1968 and 1972

69 Michael Milken: Wall Street genius who ran afoul of the law
70 Martina Navratilova: tennis great
71 Richard M. Nixon (1913–93): 37th U.S. president; resigned, 1974
72 Manuel Noriega (1938–): drug-dealing dictator of Panama
73 Oliver North: "Iranscam" operative, 1986
74 Sandra D. O'Connor: first U.S. woman Supreme Court justice, 1981
75 Daniel Ortega (1945–): leftist president of Nicaragua, 1984–90
76 Lee Harvey Oswald: assassinated President Kennedy, 1963
77 Luciano Pavarotti: opera idol
78 Pelé: soccer great
79 Francis Gary Powers (1929–77): U-2 spy pilot shot down in 1960
80 Elvis Presley (1935–77): "the King" of rock 'n' roll
81 Nancy Reagan: wife of President Reagan
82 Ronald Reagan (1911–): 40th U.S. president
83 Sally Ride: first U.S. woman astronaut
84 Pete Rose: broke Ty Cobb's lifetime record of 4,195 hits
85 Jerry Rubin: 1960s radical activist
86 Jack Ruby: killed Lee Harvey Oswald, JFK's assassin, 1963
87 Anwar Sadat (1918–81): Egyptian leader who made peace with Israel
88 Saddam Hussein: dictator of Iraq, invader of Kuwait, 1990–91

89 H. Norman Schwarzkopf (1934–): U.S. commander during the Gulf War, 1990–91
90 Alan Shepard (1923–): first American in space
91 Diana Spencer, Princess of Wales (1961–): rocky marriage to Prince Charles
92 Steven Spielberg: director of blockbuster sci fi films
93 Gloria Steinem (1934–): editor of *Ms.* magazine
94 Jimmy Swaggart: TV evangelist who fell from grace
95 Margaret Thatcher (1925–): prime minster of Great Britain, 1979–90
96 Three Mile Island: near nuclear meltdown, 1979
97 John Travolta: disco star of *Saturday Night Fever*, 1977
98 Charles Van Doren: contestant who cheated on TV quiz shows, 1958
99 Barbara Walters: popular TV interviewer
100 Andy Warhol (1927?–87): inventor of "Pop Art"
101 William Westmoreland: American commander in Vietnam War
102 Bob Woodward and Carl Bernstein: *Washington Post* reporters who broke the Watergate story, 1972
103 Boris Yeltsin (1931–): leader of Russia after the fall of communism
104 Yoko Ono: wife of John Lennon
105 Frank Zappa: eccentric rock musician

History Books You and Your Family Will Enjoy

Alan Axelrod and Charles Phillips,
What Every American Should Know About American History: 200 Events That Shaped the Nation (1992).

Gorton Carruth,
What Happened When: A Chronology of Life and Events in America (1989).

Sir Winston Churchill,
History of the English-Speaking Peoples (1956-58).

S. N. Fisher and W. L. Ochsenwald,
The Middle East: A History, 4th edition (1990).

Eric Foner and John A. Garraty, editors,
The Reader's Companion to American History (1991).

John A. Garraty,
The American Nation: A History of the United States (1994).

Lorraine Glennon, editor in chief,
Our Times: The Illustrated History of the 20th Century (1995).

Christopher Haigh, editor,
The Cambridge Historical Encyclopedia of Great Britain and Ireland (1990).

Albert Hourani,
A History of the Arab Peoples (1991; reprinted 1992).

K. O. Morgan, editor,
The Oxford Illustrated History of Britain (1984).

R. R. Palmer and Joel Colton,
A History of the Modern World, 7th editon (1991).

Paul Thomas Welty,
The Asians: Their Evolving Heritage, 6th edition (1989).

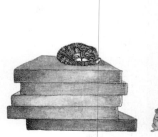

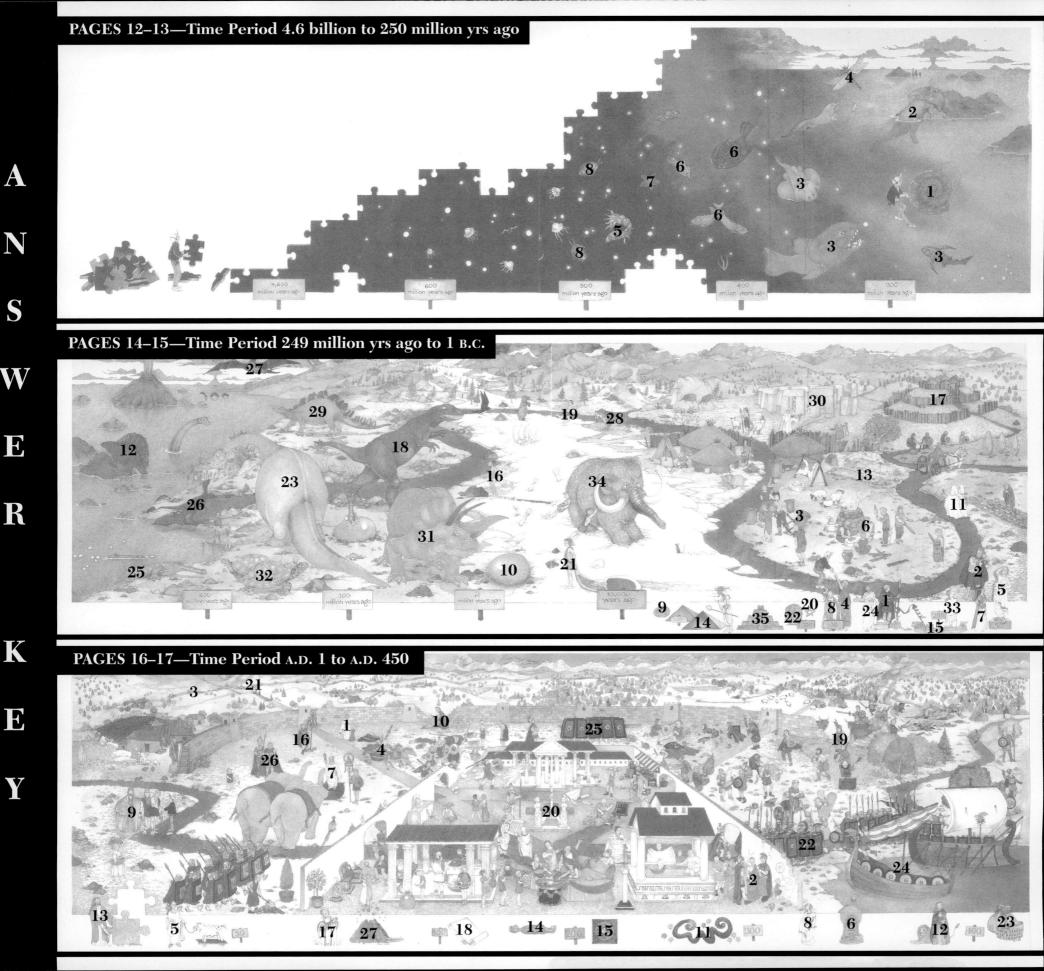

ANSWER KEY

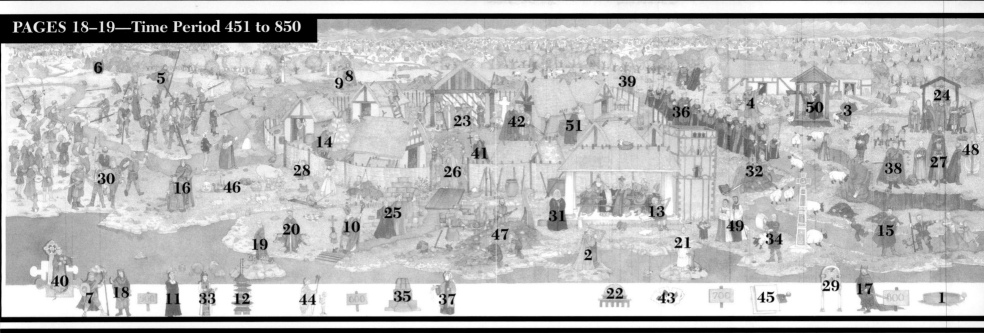

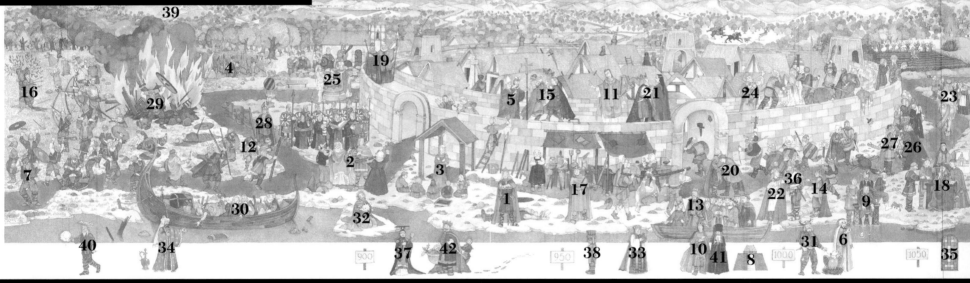

ANSWER KEY

PAGES 24–25—Time Period 1151 to 1214

PAGES 26–27—Time Period 1215 to 1309

PAGES 28–29—Time Period 1310 to 1399

PAGES 30–31—Time Period 1400 to 1460

PAGES 32–33—Time Period 1461 to 1489

PAGES 34–35—Time Period 1490 to 1549

ANSWER KEY

PAGES 36–37—Time Period 1550 to 1600

PAGES 38–39—Time Period 1601 to 1645

PAGES 40–41—Time Period 1646 to 1659

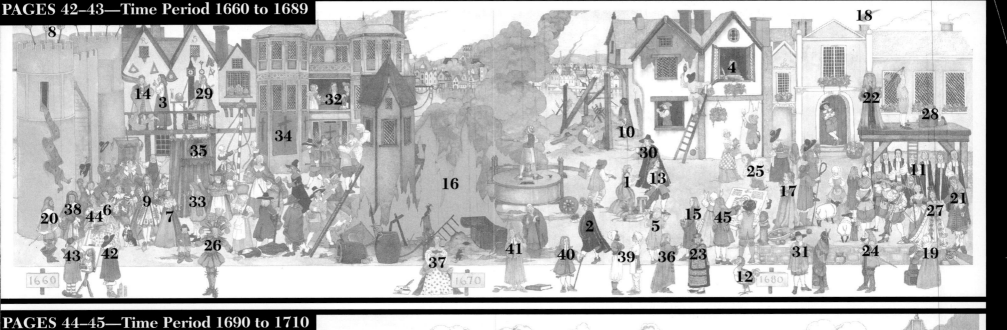

ANSWER KEY

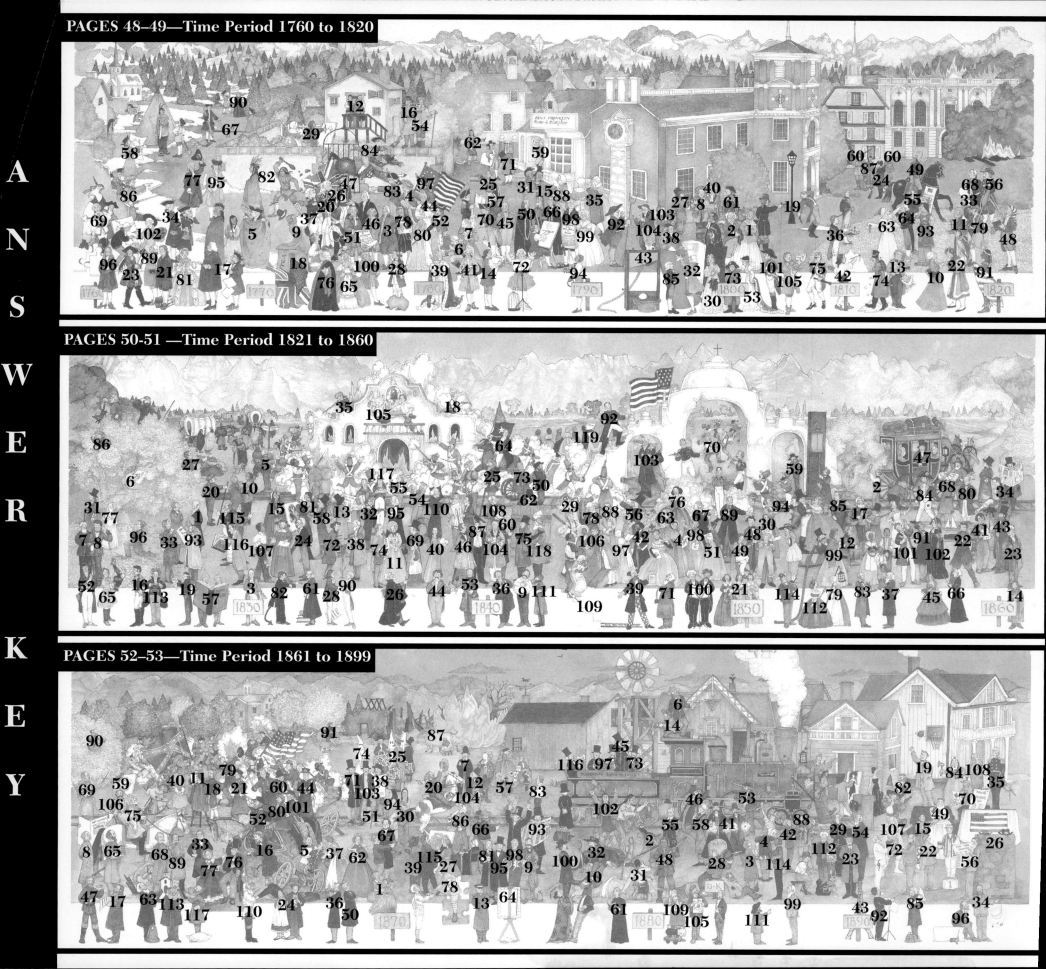

PAGES 48–49—Time Period 1760 to 1820

PAGES 50-51 —Time Period 1821 to 1860

PAGES 52–53—Time Period 1861 to 1899

ANSWER KEY

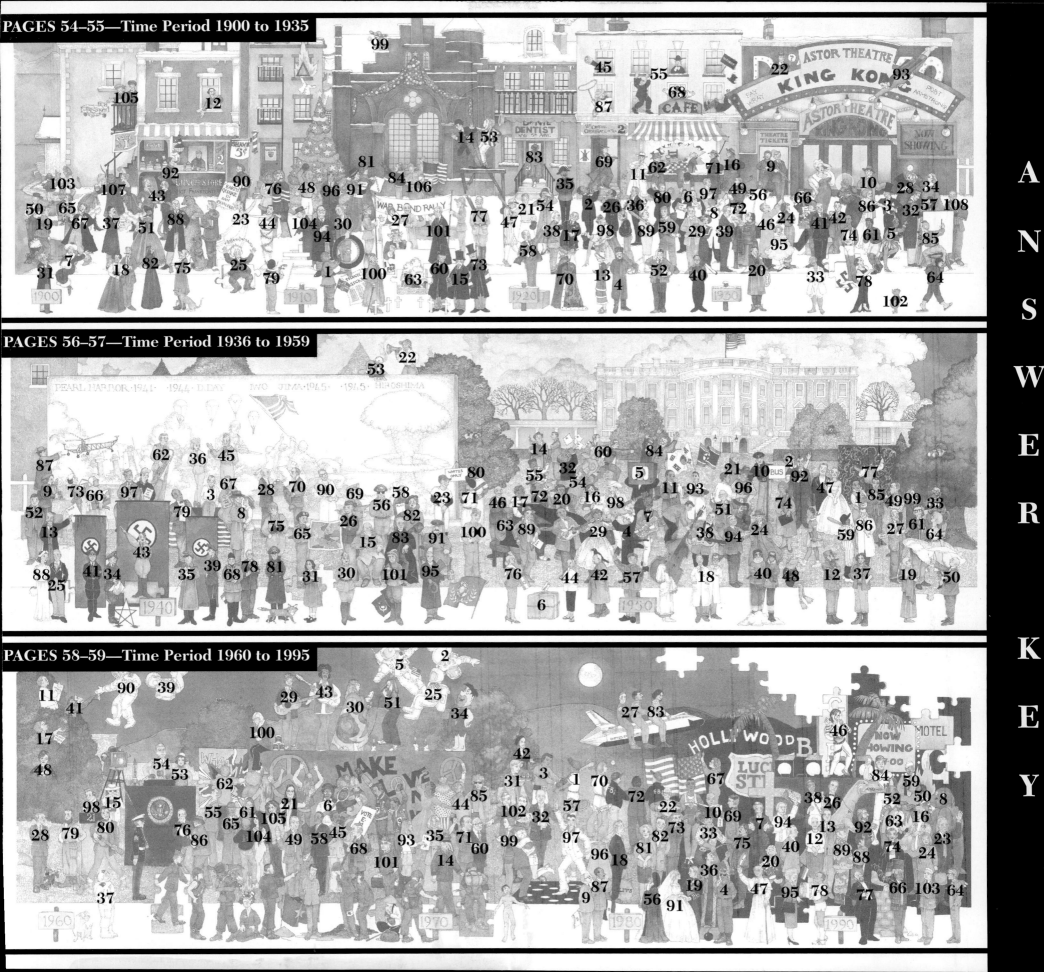

PAGES 54–55—Time Period 1900 to 1935

PAGES 56–57—Time Period 1936 to 1959

PAGES 58–59—Time Period 1960 to 1995

ANSWER KEY